CREATIVE RECIPES FOR TEA

a Salamander book
Published by Salamander Books Limited
LONDON • NEW YORK

Published by Salamander Books Ltd.,
129-137 York Way, London N7 9LG, United Kingdom.

ISBN 0 86101 612 2

Distributed by Hodder and Stoughton Services, PO Box 6, Mill Road, Dunton Green, Sevenoaks, Kent TN13 2XX.

The publishers would like to thank Crabtree & Evelyn and The Tea Council Limited

CREDITS

RECIPES BY: *Caroline Cowen, Linda Fraser, Gordon Grimsdale, Kerenza Harries, Lesley Mackley, Janice Murfitt, Jacki Passmore, Lorna Rhodes, Hilary Walden and Sally Taylor*

PHOTOGRAPHY BY: *Sue Atkinson, Per Ericson, David Gill, Paul Gruler, Alan Newnham, Jon Stewart, Alister Thorpe and Philip Wymart*

DESIGN BY: *Tim Scott*

TYPESET BY: *Maron Graphics, Wembley*

COLOUR SEPARATION BY: *P & W Graphics, Pte. Ltd.*

PRINTED IN BELGIUM BY: *Proost International Book Production, Turnhout, Belgium*

Contents

CHILLED PLUM SOUP

370 g (12 oz) red plums
125 ml (4 fl oz / ½ cup) fruity white wine
60 g (2 oz / ¼ cup) demerara sugar
2 teaspoons lemon juice
375 m (12 fl oz / 1½ cups) water
4 raspberry-flavoured tea bags
125 ml (4 fl oz / ½ cup) buttermilk
⅓ teaspoon grated lemon peel
fine lemon peel twists, to garnish

Combine plums, wine, sugar, lemon juice, and water in a saucepan. Bring to the boil, then cover and simmer gently for about 10 minutes, until tender.

Strain off juice, bring to the boil then pour over tea bags; leave to stand for 5 minutes. Press tea bags then discard. Press plums through a sieve into juice; cool. Discard skin and stones from plums.

Stir buttermilk and lemon peel into plum juice. Chill the soup in freezer for 1 hour before serving. Serve ice cold, garnished with twists of lemon peel. *Makes 4 servings*

TROUT IN ASPIC

75 ml (2½ fl oz / ⅓ cup) lemon tea
4 trout, each about 250 g (8 oz), rinsed
90 ml (3 fl oz / ⅓ cup) mayonnaise mixed with
2 teaspoons tomato purée (paste)
1 cucumber, very thinly sliced
lemon wedges, to garnish

MARINADE:

1 red onion, sliced
315 ml (10 fl oz / 1¼ cups) dry white wine
½ teaspoon each salt and black pepper

Add marinade ingredients to tea. Marinate trout in a shallow ovenproof dish for 2-3 hours. Cook trout in a preheated oven 190C (375F/Gas 5) for 15-20 minutes. Remove from oven and cool. Lift out trout and fillet. Cover trout with overlapping cucumber slices and glaze with marinade. Garnish with lemon wedges and serve with mayonnaise. *Serves 4*

APPLE & MANGO PORK

1.25 kg (2½ lb) loin of pork, boned and fat removed
4 teaspoons plain flour
155 ml (5 fl oz / ⅔ cup) water
315 ml (10 fl oz / 1¼ cups) mango tea
4 teaspoons clear honey
6 teaspoons almond oil
3 fresh bay leaves
apple slices dipped in lemon juice, to garnish
250 g (8 oz / 2 cups) prepared stuffing

Remove rind, score meat and prepare stuffing. Stir remaining ingredients into tea. Cool. Marinate pork for 4 hours. Preheat oven to 190C (375F/Gas 5). Remove meat from marinade. Pat dry. Spread stuffing over centre, roll up and tie with string. Place in roasting tin, brush with marinade and cook for 1 hour, basting. Remove meat from tin. Remove string, slice meat thinly. Garnish and serve with stuffing. *Serves 6*

Raisin Sauce

375 ml (12 fl oz / 1½ cups) boiling water
3 mango-flavoured tea bags
30 g (1 oz / ¼ cup) plain flour
1½ tablespoons light brown sugar
1½ tablespoons dry mustard
salt and freshly ground black pepper
2 tablespoons white wine vinegar
1 tablespoon lemon juice
60 g (2 oz / ⅓ cup) seedless raisins
2 tablespoons butter

In a bowl, pour half the water over the tea bags and raisins; leave to stand for 5 minutes. Press tea bags and discard. Leave raisins for a further hour. In a heavy-based saucepan, combine flour, sugar, mustard, salt and pepper. Gradually whisk in remaining boiling water to make a smooth sauce. Stir in vinegar and lemon juice then simmer gently for 3 minutes. Strain in mango tea and simmer for a further 3 minutes. Add raisins, then stir in butter. Serve hot with ham. *Makes about 440 ml (14 fl oz / 1¾ cups)*

CHOCOLATE SAUCE

315 ml (10 fl oz / 1¼ cups) milk
3 vanilla flavoured tea bags
125 g (4 oz) plain, chopped chocolate
1 teaspoon sugar
4 egg yolks, well-beaten, room temperature

In a small bowl, pour milk over tea bags; allow to stand for 5 minutes. Press tea bags and discard. In a heavy-based small saucepan over a low heat stir together milk, chocolate and sugar until smooth. Stir a little of the chocolate milk into the egg yolks, then return to heat gently, and continue stirring for 2 to 3 minutes without simmering, until thickened.

Serve hot with poached pears, ice cream, steamed puddings or soufflés. *Makes about 375 ml (12 fl oz / 1½ cups)*

BAKED APRICOTS

18 large dried apricots, about 125 g (4 oz/1 cup) total weight
1 pot freshly made Earl Grey tea
90 g (3 oz/¾ cup) ground almonds
60 g (2 oz/⅓ cup) icing sugar, sifted
60 g (2 oz) unsalted butter, melted
3 teaspoons lemon juice
18 blanched almonds
2 teaspoons sweet sherry

Put apricots in a bowl, strain hot tea over them and leave to soak overnight.

Preheat oven to 200C (400F/Gas 6).

In a bowl, mix together ground almonds, icing sugar, all but 2 teaspoons melted butter, and lemon juice. Knead to a smooth paste.

Drain apricots; pat dry with absorbent kitchen paper.

Divide almond paste into 18 pieces; press each piece around an almond and use to stuff apricots.

Brush a baking dish with remaining butter. Put apricots in dish and sprinkle with sherry. Cover with buttered paper and bake in the oven for 10 minutes. Serve hot, with chilled yogurt. *Serves 6*

TEA BAVAROIS

15 g (½ oz / 2½ teaspoons) jasmine tea
½ pt (300 ml / 1¼ cups) milk
2 eggs, separated
2 tablespoons caster sugar
1 tablespoon powdered gelatine
3 tablespoons water
185 ml (6 fl oz / ¾ cup) whipping cream
Chocolate Sauce, page 16, to serve

In a saucepan, gently heat tea in milk to boiling point. Remove from heat; leave to stand for 10-15 minutes. In a bowl, beat egg yolks and sugar until mousse-like. Slowly strain in the milk, beating. Return to saucepan over a low heat and stir until mixture coats the back of the spoon; do not let boil. Set aside. In a small bowl, sprinkle gelatine over water; let stand until softened then place over a saucepan of hot water until gelatine dissolves. Cool slightly then slowly stir into tea mixture. Cool, stirring occasionally, until thickened. Fold in cream. Whip egg whites until soft peaks form, fold into tea mixture, spoon into a lightly oiled 940 ml (30 fl oz / 3¾ cup) mould and refrigerate until set. Turn out onto a serving plate and serve with the sauce. *Serves 4-6*

WINTER COMPÔTE

125 g (4 oz / 1 cup) moist dried figs, quartered
125 g (4 oz / 1 cup) moist dried prunes
125 g (4 oz / 1 cup) no-soak dried apricots
60 g (2 oz / ½ cup) cranberries, fresh or frozen, thawed if frozen
155 ml (5 fl oz / ⅔ cup) port
155 ml (5 fl oz / ⅔ cup) China tea
pared rind and juice of ½ lemon
155 ml (5 fl oz / ⅔ cup) water
125 g (4 oz / 1 cup) ricotta cheese
2 teaspoons clear honey
30 g (1 oz / ¼ cup) toasted flaked almonds

In a saucepan, combine fruits, port, tea, lemon rind and water. Bring slowly to the boil, cover and simmer for 20 minutes. Remove from the heat and allow to cool.

When completely cold, stir in lemon juice to taste, transfer to a large bowl then chill in the refrigerator for 2 hours.

Beat together ricotta cheese, 2 teaspoons of the compôte juice and 1-2 teaspoons of honey, to taste. Spoon the compote into individual dishes, top with a spoonful of cheese mixture and decorate with the almonds. *Serves 4-6*

MOROCCAN FRUIT COMPÔTE

1.2 litres (40 fl oz/5 cups) peach-flavoured tea
125 g (4 oz/1 cup) dried whole apricots
125 g (4 oz/⅔ cup) whole pitted prunes
60 g (2 oz/⅓ cup) raisins
90 g (3 oz/⅓ cup) granulated sugar
60 g (2 oz/⅓ cup) blanched whole almonds
60 g (2 oz) unsalted butter
30 g (5 teaspoons) caster sugar
90 g (3 oz/¾ cup) plain flour, sifted
12 blanched whole almonds

Add apricots, prunes and raisins to peach-flavoured tea. Soak overnight. In a saucepan, put fruit, soaking liquid and granulated sugar. Bring to the boil, then simmer gently for 15-20 minutes. Add almonds. Transfer to a serving dish and cool. To make shortbread, preheat oven to 190C (375F/Gas 5). In a bowl, cream butter and caster sugar together until light and fluffy. Stir in flour, then mix to a firm dough; divide into 12. Roll each piece into a ball and put on a baking sheet. Press an almond onto each ball. Bake in the oven for 10 minutes. Cool on a wire rack. Serve compote with Greek yogurt and shortbread. *Serves 6*

STRAWBERRY TEA ICE CREAM

315 ml (10 fl oz / 1¼ cup) strawberry tea
2 eggs, separated, plus 4 yolks
250 g (8 oz / 1 cup) caster sugar
315 ml (10 fl oz / 1¼ cups) creamy milk
315 ml (10 fl oz / 1¼ cups) double (thick) cream, whipped
12-18 strawberries with stalks intact
185 g (6 oz / ¾ cup) prepared caramel

In a bowl, whisk egg yolks and sugar until thick and light. In a pan, heat strawberry tea and milk. Bring to the boil. Slowly pour onto egg yolk mixture, then return to pan. Heat gently, stirring constantly with a wooden spoon, until mixture thickens. Strain and cool. Fold cream into custard. Freeze until slushy, then beat thoroughly. In a separate bowl, whisk egg whites until soft peaks form; fold into ice cream. Transfer to a freezerproof container, cover, seal and freeze for about 3 hours until firm. To make caramel strawberries for decoration, grease a baking sheet. In a pan, warm caramel. Remove from heat. Dip strawberries into caramel and put on greased baking sheet to harden. Remove ice cream from freezer 30 minutes before serving, to soften. Serve decorated with strawberries. *Serves 6*

EARL GREY SORBET

470 ml (15 fl oz / 1⅞ cups) freshly made Earl Grey tea
1 lemon
a few mint leaves
90 g (3 oz / ⅓ cup) caster sugar
155 ml (5 fl oz / ⅔ cup) white wine
2 egg whites, stiffly whisked
185 g (6 oz / ¾ cup) granulated sugar

Strain tea into a bowl. Pare a few strips of rind from lemon; add to tea with mint. Add caster sugar, stirring until dissolved. Leave until cold, then stir in wine. Pour into a freezer-proof container, cover, seal and freeze for 1-1½ hours until mushy. In a food processor, process sorbet to break up ice crystals. Add egg whites to sorbet and process until well blended. Return mixture to freezer. Freeze for 1 hour, then process in food processor; repeat, then freeze for 2 hours, until firm. To make angel's hair, put granulated sugar and 155 ml (5 fl oz/⅔ cup) water in a saucepan. Heat gently until sugar has dissolved. Bring to the boil and boil rapidly, until syrup registers 155C (305F) on a sugar thermometer. Dip two forks, held back to back, into syrup. Flick over a wooden spoon handle to form threads. Serve sorbet decorated with angel's hair. *Serves 6*

Rose Petal Tea Cream

15 g (½ oz/2 tablespoons) rose pouchong tea
315 ml (10 fl oz/1¼ cups) milk
2 eggs, separated
60 g (2 oz/¼ cup) caster sugar
1 teaspoon rosewater
3 teaspoons gelatine
155 ml (5 fl oz/⅔ cup) double (thick) cream
20 clean, dry, unblemished rose petals
1 egg white, lightly beaten
caster sugar

Brush rose petals with egg white. Gently toss in caster sugar until completely coated. Dry on a wire rack. In a saucepan, bring tea and milk to the boil. Remove from the heat and infuse for 5 minutes. In a bowl, whisk together egg yolks and caster sugar. Strain tea-flavoured milk onto egg yolk mixture; stir in rosewater. Dissolve gelatine in 3 tablespoons water; stir into tea mixture. Chill until just beginning to set. In a bowl, whip cream; fold into tea mixture. In a clean bowl, whisk egg whites until soft peaks form; gently fold into tea mixture. Turn into 4 wetted 185 ml (6 fl oz/¾ cup) individual jelly moulds. Chill for 2-3 hours, until set. Turn out onto serving plates. Decorate with crystallized rose petals. *Serves 4*

GLOSSY FRUIT LOAF

60 g (2 oz / 1/3 cup) raisins
60 g (2 oz / 1/3 cup) chopped dates
90 ml (3 fl oz / 1/3 cup) cold Assam tea
125 g (4 oz) unsalted butter
125 g (4oz / 3/4 cup) light soft brown sugar
2 eggs, beaten
185 g (6 oz / 1 1/2 cups) self-raising flour, sifted
90 g (3 oz / 1/2 cup) glacé cherries, halved
90 g (3 oz / 3/4 cup) coarsely chopped Brazil nuts
30 g (1 oz / 1/3 cup) walnut halves
60 g (2 oz / 1/3 cup) glacé cherries, halved
6 teaspoons apricot jam, sieved

Put raisins and dates in a bowl, pour over tea, cover and leave to soak overnight. Preheat oven to 160C (325F/Gas 3). Grease and line a 1 kg (2 lb) loaf tin. In a bowl, cream together butter and sugar until light and fluffy. Gradually add eggs, then fold in flour alternately with soaked fruit. Gently stir in cherries and chopped nuts. Turn into prepared tin and arrange walnuts and cherries on top. Bake in the oven for 1½-1¾ hours, until a skewer inserted into the centre of the cake comes out clean. Transfer to a wire rack to cool. Glaze top with apricot jam. *Serves 10*

JAPANESE GREEN TEA ICE

60 ml (2 fl oz / ¼ cup) boiling water
1¼ tablespoons Japanese green tea leaves
2 egg whites
155 g (5 oz / 1 cup) icing sugar
1 egg yolk
375 ml (12 fl oz / 1½ cups) whipping cream
green food colouring, if desired

In a small bowl, pour boiling water over tea leaves. Steep until cold. Strain tea liquid.

In a small bowl, beat egg whites to soft peaks. Add sugar, 1 tablespoon at a time. Beat in egg yolk, then cooled tea liquid.

In a small bowl, beat cream to soft peaks. Fold into ice. If desired, add 2 to 3 drops colouring.

Pour into several undivided ice trays; cover; place in freezer, freeze until firm. *Makes 6 servings*

PEPPERMINT TEA SORBET

500 ml (16 fl oz/2 cups) water
15 g (½ oz/¼ cup) peppermint tea leaves
125 ml (4 fl oz/½ cup) sugar syrup, see below
lemon slices and mint leaves, to garnish, if desired

In a small saucepan, boil water; add tea leaves. Cover and steep 3 hours. Strain through a fine nylon sieve.

Mix tea liquid and sugar syrup. Pour into an ice cream container. Freeze in ice cream maker according to manufacturer's directions.

FREEZER METHOD: Pour prepared mixture into several undivided ice trays. Place in freezer; freeze to a slush.

In a food processor/blender process semi-frozen sorbet 1 minute or until light. Return to trays; cover; freeze until firm.

Garnish with slices of lemon and mint leaves, if desired.

To make *Sugar Syrup*, in a large saucepan bring 1 kg (2 lb) caster (superfine) sugar and 950 ml (32 fl oz/4 cups) water to a gentle boil. Reduce heat and simmer for 10 minutes. Remove from heat and cool before using. Store, refrigerated, for up to 3 weeks. *Makes 6 servings*

BANANA-TEA MILK SHAKE

500 ml (16 fl oz/2 cups) boiling milk
2 mango-flavoured tea bags
2 ripe bananas
2 tablespoons natural (plain) yogurt
1-2 tablespoons caster sugar

In a bowl, pour the milk over the tea bags, cover and let stand for 2-3 minutes. Press the bags, then discard. Cool the milk, then refrigerate. Peel and chop bananas, reserving a few slices for decoration. In a food processor or blender, mix bananas, milk and yogurt. Add caster sugar to taste. Pour into cold glasses and decorate with reserved banana slices. Serve at once with wide straws. *Makes about 500 ml (16 fl oz/2 cups)*

ROSE PETAL INFUSION

3 rosehip tea bags
315 ml (10 fl oz / 1¼ cups) boiling water
6-9 teaspoons rosehip syrup
handful scented rose petals
9 teaspoons triple distilled rosewater
625 ml (20 fl oz / 2½ cups) sparkling mineral water
ice cubes
rose petals, to decorate

Put tea bags into a bowl and pour over the boiling water. Leave to infuse for 10 minutes, then remove tea bags and leave liquid to cool.

When completely cold, stir in rosehip syrup, rose petals and rosewater and leave to infuse for a further 30 minutes. Strain and add mineral water.

Fill tall glasses with ice cubes, pour over the rose petal infusion and decorate with petals. *Serves 4-6*

Souchon Punch

1 Lapsang Souchon tea bag
625 ml (20 fl oz / 2½ cups) boiling water
4 teaspoons light soft brown sugar
315 ml (10 fl oz / 1¼ cups) clear apple juice
90 ml (3 fl oz / ⅓ cup) bourbon or brandy
2 lemon slices
3 lime slices
625 ml (20 fl oz / 2½ cups) American dry ginger ale
ice cubes
lemon geranium leaves
lemon and lime peel spirals, to garnish

Place tea bag in a jug and pour on the boiling water. Infuse for 4-5 minutes without stirring, then remove tea bag. Stir in sugar and leave until cold. Pour tea into a large glass bowl, add apple juice, bourbon or brandy and lemon and lime slices.

Just before serving, add ginger ale, ice cubes and lemon geranium leaves. Stir well and serve garnished with spirals of lemon and lime peel. *Serves 12*

SPICED ORANGE TEA

1 large orange
4 cloves
1 cinnamon stick
250 ml (8 fl oz/1 cup) fresh orange juice
500 ml (16 fl oz/2 cups) Lapsang Souchong tea
3-6 teaspoons clear honey
125 ml (4 fl oz/½ cup) pineapple juice
½ teaspoon freshly grated nutmeg
slices of orange and freshly grated nutmeg, to garnish

Stud the orange with cloves, prick it all over and put into a saucepan with cinnamon and orange juice. Bring to the boil and simmer for 5 minutes. Remove from the heat and allow to infuse for 30 minutes in the pan. Remove the orange and spices and add the tea and honey to taste. Stir in pineapple juice and nutmeg and reheat gently. Pour into heatproof glasses and garnish with slices of orange and a sprinkling of freshly grated nutmeg. *Serves 4*